Business Plan: For Startup & Small Business Success Today!

SADANAND PUJARI

Published by SADANAND PUJARI, 2024.

Table of Contents

Copyright 1

About 2

Introduction 3

Just One Second! 4

What Is A Business Plan? 5

Viewing The 5 Parts Briefly 7

Introduction To The Executive Summary 8

What To Include In Your Executive Summary 9

Introduction To The Marketing Plan 13

What To Include In Your Marketing Section 14

I Need A Favor Please! 19

Introduction To The Operations Plan 20

What To Include In Your Operations Section 21

Introduction To The Financial Plan 25

What To Include In Your Financial Section 26

Introduction To Appendices 29

What To Include In This Section 30

I Need A Favor Please! 32

Recap 33

5 Ways To Improve Your Cash Flow Forecast 34

An Introduction To Cash Flow Forecasting 37

How To Close More Sales 44

What Next 48

Copyright

Copyright © 2024 by **SADANAND PUJARI**

All rights reserved. No part of this book may be reproduced, scanned, or distributed in any printed or electronic form without permission. Please do not participate in or encourage piracy of copyrighted materials in violation of the author's rights. Purchase only authorised editions.

Business Plan: For Startup & Small Business Success Today!

Business Planning Success Can Be Easily Achieved By Using This Comprehensive Business Plan

First Edition: Jun 2024

Book Design by **SADANAND PUJARI**

About

Whenever the word "Business Plan" is mentioned most people freeze! What follows are the words "I don't know how to write one". In reality it needs not be this way.

That is why I have taken the lid off and delivered these chapters in plain English that need to be considered and included within a business plan. This Book has been designed to help those who are writing plans for the first time or for those who write business plans infrequently (Even seasoned business plan writers will learn one or two things, I promise!) . I want you to know that the information contained in this Book has been used to help many start-up and growing businesses and I am confident it will be of tremendous value to you.

I am confident of a useful outcome for you! So what are you waiting for? Every delay is a barrier stopping you from starting and running a successful business. Sign Up Now!

Introduction

You're welcome in this Book. I'm going to teach you the exact business plan templates and I used to write over 40 successful business plans. We are going to consider three vital aspects of a business plan. Number one we're going to consider the structure of our business.

Secondly we're going to explore the important information that you need to include in your business plan. And thirdly you're going to use this time to persuade yourself and investors or other people you're going to be working with that you actually have a viable business.

In a nutshell you're going to end up with what I call the approved business plan and I'm hoping you can learn all this in one hour. So let's get straight into the Book.

Just One Second!

Just one second. Who did this go over to the discussion area which is on the right side of the screen and write your name the country you're from or what you hope to get out of this Book so that I can get to know you and other students and also get to know you and add value to your experience on the Book. Now let's go straight in.

What Is A Business Plan?

In this chapter I want to give you a broad definition of what a business plan is without complicating matters of tone. Just laying in bed playing with a business plan is a document that details your cake and eat which is paid for knowledge. So you've gathered up all this amount of information from your research and your discussions and now you're going to put that into a strategic plan then you're going to execute. So your business plan is a combination of that knowledge you gain the strategy you're going to take which is what we think about strategy. A strategy really is a plan of action that you've designed to achieve a long term objective. So what actions you're going to take plus the execution part of it is the order of that action. So if you think about it like that it makes it really plain and easy to understand what the business plan is. The man explained to you in another way a business plan is a document detailing what you're going to do, why you're going to do it and how you're going to do it.

So go read and there is the information you've gained from researching your market and then why you decided that after you've looked at your market you decided OK this is what you're going to do. That's why sometimes you call your USP because your decision to take certain kinds of action and plans is what actually gives you your unique selling proposition. So I'll tell you what you're going to do, which is after research, to get the information. They decide where you're going to run your business in this particular manner. And then the final part is how you plan to do it at this point. I always tell people if I'm delivering this in seven hours since people say after me that my business plan is easy to write or I might say writing a business plan is easy. After me writing a business plan is easy. All right. I'll see you in the next chapter.

There's no question about the number of different types of templates that you can use to write your business. If you went to a bank for example that might give you their own templates different bands have different templates different agencies have different templates. It's not a problem I say because the template I'm going to give you is a template that I've used to write over 40 business plans and what I've discovered over the years and I've used this template is that if I get a different template from an investor or from a bank I could easily cut and paste the information that I've got on my templates into that template.

So don't worry about it if the template I'm going to give you now is different. But one thing I guarantee you is that it works. It gives all the information you need and gets you going very quickly. So in this chapter I'm going to give you a brief overview of what I call the five parts to a successful business plan.

Viewing The 5 Parts Briefly

In this chapter I want to show you the five parts of your business plan. Now in order to capture the important details you've got to follow these five parts to a business plan. The first part is the executive summary. The second part is the marketing plan. The third part is the operation plan. Then the financial plan and finally the executive summary should summarize the whole plan in about 2 pages.

The marketing plan explores the market going into the products you're going to sell and how you plan to meet your market. The operations plan is how the business plans to operate itself within the given market. The financial plan is really about the money matters and the appendices covers extra information or extra supporting information that should be included in the plan. So I'll see you in the next chapter as we begin to explore each of these five parts in greater detail.

Introduction To The Executive Summary

That we're going to explore the executive summary legs. The summary is sometimes called the Business Plan Summary or just a summary and is supposed to give the reader a quick snapshot of what your business intends to do and how you intend to go about doing it. It is true and you've heard that the executive summary is probably the two most important pages that somebody will read of business. They want to make it interesting and we're making good. We want to make it. I actually want to make it snappy if you want to make it work for the purpose for which your vision is. So I'm going to give you a form of the reviews as always got the results desired. So I will see you at the chapter.

What To Include In Your Executive Summary

I'm using this particular image because it adequately illustrates what I'm trying to portray to you in regards to the executive summary. Now the executive summary is one of the most important parts of your business plan and I want to suggest to you right up front that you're right this part of the business plan last. The reason is that some of the information you need you will not have it on till you've finished your plan or near financial plan. So you'll write your executive summary. Plus the second vital point that I want to make is that your executive summary must be interesting enough for anyone who reads it. Now think about this if you're going for funding. Investors receive around about a thousand business plans a month. That means the region has time to read stuff that doesn't interest them.

So you've got to give them exactly what they want to hear you want to give it to them straight with no fluff talk. So I'm going to show you how to write a winning executive summary. So let's get started. The first chapter of the executive summary I want to use headings for is we want to talk about your background and experience and then include a summarized version of your management team. Now here's the deal. If you've worked in any area of industry you're going into then you want to detail the experience there. If you've not worked in the industry but you've had employment that aligns with the type of work you'll be doing in this new business then you want to write about it instead.

So either way that's gonna be something in that background and experience that pops to the investors or the people that you want to come along or even to yourself as a way of reassuring yourself that you have some experience to run a business. The other thing is now you must include a summarized version of your management team. Just talk about what the management team has done for you since they started helping you out and what kind of results have they got, what experience do they have just a summarized version. I'll talk about this as we look at the operations plan in a moment. The second chapter of the executive summary is the Naish problem the product and sales Naish problem products and sales.

So let me then we'll talk about it one by one. The Naish Do not be like most people who want to sell a product to every single person on earth even Coca-Cola doesn't do that. There are some people who would never drink Coca-Cola and that's a big huge brand. There are some people who don't wear Nike. Some people don't wear Jordans. Some people don't buy DVDs; your products will not work for everyone. Particularly in the beginning you want to have a niche. They are selling too. So what they need is a chapter of the potential market. You could be selling too. So let's just think about Google. All of us now use Google for searches. I think so. But think about this when Google first started I wasn't even good on the internet.

I probably wasn't savvy enough to even go do a search or perhaps some people one of whom was born here but Google too in that business too was the niche the particular group of people that needed me at that time knowing that they're going to scale up. I know you're going to scale up and you're going to sell to millions of people who are the first few hundreds you got to sell to or the first few 10 people you're going to sell to. What their age group was the level of income where you live. Can you put together a profile of those people? Now you did talk about that Naish. So it could be I'm aiming at selling my product to the 25 to 35 year olds that live in a particular area and have this type of problem that I want to solve. So what's the problem you're solving for that group? And then what's the product you've created to solve that problem.

Now the sales part of it is the proof that you have the right Naish that you're selling to. You've got a wrap problem that you're solving and you've got the right products for that particular need. And you made some sales. Now when I talk about sales here I'm not talking about you haven't sold a million units of whatever you're selling. That's not the point. The point is you sold this product to 10 people and you saw this for up to five people. I sold it to 20 people. Just enough sales that shows the investors or shows yourself that confirms to you as an entrepreneur that you are doing the right business or that this business will make money. It's a money making business.

It is not a money making business. How many people have used your services over the past two months that you started and we tested is what you will be testing later on. Most important to write about this in your executive summary the chapter you want to write about your executive summary is the risks and solutions the risk and solution. So what solution do you have for the risks that are eminent in your business? So for example if you think about driving traffic to a Geo Web site as the means of generating sales that's a huge risk. So what happens if the traffic doesn't come? What other plans do you have? What are the solutions you have or the solution you have to overcome the risk of the risk that you are facing. So you could talk about that as well here. Every business has a risk and do not say to yourself oh this business has no risk you know that's going to make you serious.

The fourth chapter of your executive summary is the amount of money you expected or expected. Profits in the first 12 months. So there was going to be an expected profit if you wrote a particular figure and this Figo you can only get it from your previous account or from the actual focus. That's one of the reasons why I said that you should write this executive summary last. And then finally you can talk about how much you need you're going to have a specific figure as to how much you think you need to start this business up and running. Sometimes you're talking to an enterprise and you say well okay I'm a junior. While I go now I think I'm going to need $10000 or I think I'm going to need $15000 but I don't know I'm not sure what I'm going to cut it. What's going to cut is you first of all have an amount in mind which you can get from a cash flow forecast.

And by the way I'm going to give you a cash flow template that you're going to use to calculate your cash flow as long as you have all the figures you automatically do for you. So that way to stress yourself about trying to come up with a figure just put in the costs and income you plan to make and you ultimately calculate the figure for from that you get a profit loss account. That also shows you exactly how much you need. You might have to tweak it a bit but it works and is good. So and great, discover exactly how much you need and the amount of money should be written in your executive summary. So then they go away again. I think they're going to write about your background and experience including a summarized version of your management team. And the second one as a heading is you finish the problem, the part of the sales you generated and also the risks and solution. And then the expected profit. And finally how much you need for your business. All right, I'll see you in the next chapter.

Introduction To The Marketing Plan

Now we're going to consider the marketing plan you're going to hear me say that if your marketing plan is wrong then the whole business plan is wrong. That's how crucial it is to get your marketing plan right. It is the part of the plane that loops outside of your business. It takes your product into the marketplace, tests your product with potential clients and determines how you are going to reach those kinds and scale up your business. It's an extremely important part of the plan to get straight into it.

What To Include In Your Marketing Section

Someone once told me that the marketing plan is like the legs that the chair is standing on. If the legs are faulty then the whole chair is going to collapse. So if you think about it like that if your marketing plan is wrong then exactly some of the wrong operations plan would be wrong. Your financial planner will also be wrong. So your marketing plan is such a vital part of the business plan. It is the area that talks about what you want to do, what it is you are looking to do. So let's get straight into it and talk about how to document this and do your research.

The first area of research is really about testing your product now. You've chosen the niche now to choose a Naish. It's difficult. People think your name should be a group of people you are familiar with, a group of people you love or a group of people that you are familiar with their needs so as to be a group of people you know, a group of people you love or who you are familiar with.

Well just think about that. Think about the people that you're familiar with the people that you've been working with or you've been working with within the particular industry people you love could be you know your type of age group or people you know could be a group of friends or a group of young people or older people that you've come to know over the years or a part of that you know over the years maybe because it's been a hobby before and they want to take it to a business. So when you think about your Naish you should be thinking about a small group of people that you're going to sell your products too fast and following on from that analysis is moving into testing your product and to test the product. You've got to create what I call a minimum viable product. A minimum viable product is the minimum solution that your ideal or potential customers are willing to pay for.

That solves their problems. A minimum viable product will be something like If you want to create a self-help book for those who want to lose weight. So it may not be a thousand page book. It can just talk about the food to eat and the exercise to take. And the way to exercise it. So it could be that those three things may be that the particular group you're aiming for are willing to pay for X because it's a minimum viable product. Everything else is detailed. Maybe they don't want to just want that right. So you could test your minimum viable products and talk about that. The next thing you want to do in your marketing plan is generating some sales. Like I said in the executive summary generating sales does not mean you are selling millions of units. That's going to come later when you scale up.

But initially you want to determine how much sail you are going to make. You want to start making some sales to prove to yourself that this business is viable. It also proves to yourself that you're reaching your niche market. We're going to look at promotions companies the moment the only way you're going to be able to put together a promotion campaign that talks about how you're going to reach your potential clients is because you have unleash And you know where that niche market is. And you know how to reach that particular group of people without knowing that you're not going to meet any sales, so part of generating sales is actually your proof that your business will work. So you need to sell some of your products. At this stage before you finish a business plan then you now begin to look at your competitors.

There's an argument about whether you should detail your competitors first or your competitors. Well I would suggest you do both at the same time. Because if you look at your competitors fast you may be carried away with what they're doing. And then that might limit your creativity. But then if you don't look at your competitors you may miss out on some vital information because your competitors can actually show you what is working in the market. I suggest you select the Naish tester part that you have in mind to look at how your competitors do this three at the same time or in the order of First you create your Praag ops and then you look at what your competitors are doing. Either way, whatever steps you choose to take, you have to document your competitors. And I would suggest you look at your competitors from three levels.

The competitor that is doing that is maybe 20 years ahead of you. One there is 10 years ahead of you and one that is only about three to five years ahead of you. So you want to look at those competitors and analyze them without using SWAT's strengths, weaknesses, opportunities and threats. What are they doing? Well what is it they need to improve and what opportunities are they missing out on that you can capitalize on or what threats are facing them that you can capitalize on. So you want to think about it like you want to go to that Website. You want to find all the literature they have and you want to read it and really look at them and understand them. What products are they selling? How much are they selling their products?

They go in after and how much money they make. You will be able to use all the information to help you to come up with your own unique selling point but you're not relying on that because you've got your own ideas that you are testing as well. So that's why there's a thought between where to look at competitors first or to test the process. I suggest my thing would be Tessmacher for us because I believe in my own ideas. That's one of the ways. But you may choose to look at competitors first. It really doesn't matter. But as you document your plan you've got to talk about what you've tested sales generated. You've got to talk about your competitors as well. Number four is now you decide on how much you're going to charge for a product, what kind of promotion you are going to employ and what products you're going to create. Now you may start by only creating one product and that's ok.

Knowing that as your market grows you're going to create more products or as you see fit you're going to create more products in terms of promotion. I talked about that earlier on. How do you plan to reach your initial market and always choose the best and the cheapest promotions to run? You know initially there's not much money. So always choose the best and the cheapest one of the things that the internet affords us is you can test whether a promotion company is going to work by just spending $10 $5 on Facebook $10 each year actual two or three days you would know whether you are going to work or not where you would know whether people are interested in your product or not. That's the way you're going to do it.

Spend a little amount in the beginning and then you can spend more. As you know you're comparing walls and then price. You know when we talk about new businesses in particular the first thing people think about is to compete on price. Well OK you can compete on price but it's not the only thing to compete on. You can compete on quality, you can compete on delivery, you can compete on after sales. Instead of thinking about competing on price. Price is not the only thing to compete on. Actually you can charge more for your product because you want to use that as a differentiating factor in the market so that you appeal to another group of people that like paying more for a higher quality kind of service or product. Don't always think about dropping your price but to the price that you know they are knish can afford to pay. And then finally you're going to create a portion of a campaign.

I suggest you create an eight weeks promotional campaign that looks OK when I from where I'm at right now I tested my product. So next week I'm going to do it. I want to take it up a notch and make it possible to create my web now. Then I'm going to stop promoting to a group outside of my sphere of influence and sell to people in a particular location whatever you're going to do in the eight weeks promotional campaign and you can find copies of the hour. Actually I'll try and provide you with an example so you can see the eight weeks promotional campaign so they understand how it works. That's what you're going to do with your marketing plan. Once you've researched in this manner and you've documented it you're going to realize that you have a formidable marketing plan. How soon is the next chapter?

I Need A Favor Please!

Hi there I know a favorite place if you've got a lot of value from the Book. Could you please post a review. Does that click in the number of stars you think the Book dissolves will be just good enough for now so that when you actually finish the Book then you can go back in and if you want it to last you have the intention to post reviews. But one of the things the co-authors sometimes forget so that's why I'm asking you now to please post the review. Thanks so much. That's what you said.

Introduction To The Operations Plan

There is a saying that charity begins at home. This is the part of your business plan that actually ensures you get your home in order. So this area considers We ask something that fits your business plan in turn. That's why it's called an operation. Now let's get straight into it.

What To Include In Your Operations Section

When we talk about the marketing plan we looked at we looked at the knish we're trying to reach and a can of promotion we're going to do and how we're going to investigate our competitors. So we're looking outwards now. The operations plan looks to go back to the KSC that I talked about earlier, the knowledge strategy and execution. This is the part of execution where the rubber meets the road so to speak in your organization. How do you plan to organize yourself so that you can execute correctly or execute effectively? So let's get started. Now the first area that you want to document that you think about that you want to really seek advice for is the area of your business structure.

What type of business structure are you going to have? I'm not talking about the organizational structure that you can think about here as well. But I'm really referring to the business structure that relates to your tax position. So are you going to be an LLC or a sole proprietorship or a partnership or are you going to be a limited company in the UK. What type of business structure you can have. Sometimes before people do anything else they go to a website they go. Sarah Palin Media a company that's a wrong way of running the business particularly for the first time when you want to do a test to make sure you identify the problem. Make sure you have the minimum viable product.

Make sure you generate one or two sales before you start doing that. So this is why the operations come after the marketing plan. Right. You have to think about what type of business structure you're going to have. One of the ways to look at it is how much money do you plan to generate in the first 12 months and you don't need to worry too much about this particularly if you're going to investors investors will tell you they'll let you know what kind of business structure they need to have. Don't lose sleep over it but just understand that particularly if you're in this business for yourself you don't need anybody else's money. You gotta be thinking about how much money I plan to make in the first year before I decide on the kind of business I'm going to have.

Because really when you think about it particularly in the UK if you're a self-employed person or because sole traders are what we call self or self assessments then you can really just tap that up without paying anybody any money. And you just register with the HMRC and off you go. But if you're in a limited company and you don't know how to register with the forms you can use an accountant and that's going to cost you some money. But do you really need that in the beginning? Just part of the sole trader and you can always come virtually to the company. But if you're starting with three people and you want anybody to know what amount of shares each person owns because we're putting in an amount of money then you didn't intercompany. So you can all own shares in the enterprise.

So those are some of the things you should do and you think about what are the advantages of the you've chosen to take and what are the disadvantages or why have you chosen to do things this way. That's the business structure in a nutshell that you want to talk about your management team in full. You want to look at OK since they've been the management team, what contribution they made to your business, what contacts have they brought into your business and how well they compliment your own skills. Having a management team for my team's sake is really rubbish. You want to look at people who compliment you and who can add value to what you're doing and your management team needs to prove that they are going to help you get further than you can yourself.

You can write about the experience when you've achieved and how they've helped you. I used to be documented in this place. The third area to look at is the area of insurance. What kind of insurance are you going to have that's going to help to comply with the legal framework that your country has or is necessary for that particular kind of business? Do you need to have it as a liability ? Do you need to have firearm theft third party insurance? Be careful about having loss of profits, kind of insurance that just costs a fortune. You want to limit the amount of expenses you have and so I would suggest only being legally compliant with the insurance. And then as the business grows then you can take out other types of insurance. Then we talk about virtual stuff.

So I always say to new entrepreneurs that rather than employ somebody, get them to have a contract so that they're working on a fixed amount of money or get virtual stuff for the same type of work. You get someone in India now. That's what I learned recently that a company in the UK a blue chip company in the UK flew over to London six accountants from India put them up in a hotel for two weeks pay them their wages flew them back to India and it cost them less than they will have paid if they hired a firm in the UK. Now that's amazing. You bring people with the same amount of expertise that just shows that the world is so different and you can get stuff from all over the world that are going to help your business to grow. You don't need to employ somebody if you do not have to only employ somebody that you've tested you've tried you've tested them and they can have real value to your business.

When you think about your management team as well you could postpone any kind of payments to them if they're going to add value to you and they will like what you're doing. They'll do it if you can afford to pay them and do pay them. But when it comes to staffing don't jump in as the employed people you're asking for trouble. If you do that and then the final chapter of your operations plan to focus on the person or development training that you plan to have as a person as an entrepreneur I need to be growing either by reading books, attending seminars, doing some exhibitions or going to some trade fairs. You need to be growing and need to be improving. So if it's two three of you're in the business what kind of person development training do you plan to have. How much is it going to cost?

Remember all this from the marketing plan to the operations. Some of these items will cost you money which we're going to take into the financial plan. That's how we develop our financial plan because we're looking at exactly how much it's going to cost to have that insurance, how much it's going to cost to use the virtual staff and how much is my training going to cost because I need to include that in my cash flow and preventative care. So I'll see you in the next chapter. That's what you need to do to document all the information necessary for your operations plan. See you in the next election.

Introduction To The Financial Plan

You can have a well written business plan in terms of content. Part numbers play a big part when it comes to writing this and you've got to get that right. You've got to import all your costs that you assume will be spent into a financial structure that you can understand and anyone else will in your business plan and also and that is why we call this chapter the financial plan. This is the place where you begin to discover exactly how much it's going to cost you to run your business.

What To Include In Your Financial Section

Now we come to the part where most people love finance. Yeah. OK. Pull up part of the plan. So even if you feel you don't like it you cannot get out of it. And you know over the years I've come to like it because it's actually easy to do with the temperature. I'm going to give it to you. So don't worry about it. Just remember my business plan is easy to create. Right remember that your financial plan is the place where you bring in all the costs of every item you've mentioned throughout your business plan you've got to bring those figures into your financial plans. Sometimes investors will read your executive summary and they'll come straight into your financial plan and start digging into your financial plan because they expect to find something wrong with it.

But it doesn't have to be that way. They're just questioning whether you've really thought about it in a financial way exactly what your business will cost. So let's go straight into the financial plan. One of the items you might want to include in your financial plan section is budget. Exactly how much do you need to spend per month for a person or budget. How much are your arrangements to transport? How much are you likely to withdraw from the business on a month by month basis? The second most important area of the financial plan is actually a cash flow forecast. Now somebody says your son talks about the past. Your balance sheet is a present and your cash flow is the future. This is really looking at how much you plan to spend over the next 12 months. It's the inflow and outflow of money from your business.

How much do you plan to make this month? How much do you plan to spend this month and what's going to be the difference. Are you going to need extra support like overdraft or a loan to tide you over. Why should getting the money in this is really important if it's selling on invoice basis. You sell in January the first but you don't get paid until February the 1st. So you have a four week gap. You don't recall that as money in because you've not actually received the money. Even though that sale will go into your account it will not show your cash flow but you might have expenses in that said January. So you need to include that in a cash flow forecast. And if you don't have enough then that shows you need a supperless from somewhere either overdraft in the loan to tide you over until you get the money on the first of February.

That's how cash flow works is really interesting. But you've got to come to the cash flow forecast template with the figures yourself. Nobody's going to cover the figures for you to think about the figures they're going to come up with as close as you can. Don't worry if it's not perfect and it's to be as close as you can then after you finish your cash flow forecast you should actually write what's called Notes for cash flow. For example, I just talked about it here. He might say I'm going to make this amount of sales in January but I don't get paid until a month after. So the way I'm selling my product means I'm going to be owed money every four weeks. So that's why I need the loan of an investment.

You might also write with an. Build a website with a built in month one within a built in month five and it's going to cost this money. But we're going to be with Phase 1 in month 5. Phase 2 in month 7 and Phase 3 in Montreux. So just explain that when somebody is looking at the item on your cash for caulkers. They can see exactly what you're talking about and how you plan to spend the money but make sure whatever item you put in your marketing plan or operations plan. Making sure you input those figures into your financial plan is absolutely important. And there are no gaps. This is where people get in trouble because if you mention something in a business plan say in your campaign you've suggested you're going to have a Facebook campaign that you're going to run for maybe six months and then somebody comes to your cash flow forecasts and they cannot find an item that talks about promotion or all we like. Okay.

And what you said and what your finances say is very different. How do we know you are on the side to run a business if you can import your expenses accurately. So you want to be careful about that. And then with the template I'm going to give you it automatically calculates for you the profit and loss account. So you don't need to worry about that he might tweak it a bit but it really does it for him. Remember what's most important actually is cash flow. If you're in business, your cash flow is more important than your professional account. My template would absolutely definitely do that for you. So look out for it in the next picture. So our season.

Introduction To Appendices

For those of us who like football, what the Americans call soccer, you'll discover that players with the reserve team can actually deliver you from trouble. You might bring someone on to replace an existing player and that person you bring on goes to score a goal within the first two or three minutes. That's how useful a reserve team can be in the same way your appendices can be just as important to your business plan as we're going to discover in a minute.

What To Include In This Section

This is the final part. And also a useful chapter of the business plan is called the appendices This is where you download. Put a lot of information that you think is too bulky to be placed in the actual business plan. You could put it on the back here and title it appendices. So let's see what needs to be in there. Number one is your recent CV. Now don't ask me why but many investors want to have a look at your CV. Perhaps they want to have a look at your timeline and see your progression or they might be looking for information that helps them to understand you and know you better. So it's nice to put a recent CV in there.

Now what about letters of intent. I've seen these letters of intent to be a game changer particularly when it comes to raising money from investors. I remember sitting in a committee where we were giving people loans. I remember that when we changed our minds that day was the fact that somebody came up with intense letters of intense letters that have been written by potential customers stating that they will purchase from you when you start your business. That could be a very powerful tool in your hands. So you need to work on getting lessons of intent. At least three to ten because of intent that could help you change the game when it comes to raising money. Limit three letters of recommendation.

If you do not have lessons of intent you might have letters of recommendation from people that you've worked with before. People who know you. Maybe you've done some work in the community and a community leader writes about us. Those are also letters that help to show your character, your zeal and your contribution. People love that. And then finally supporting documents should also be placed in this chapter. What kind of supporting documents am I talking about when

I'm talking about statistics that relate to the garnish or stats that relate to your market or stats that relate to your products.

What ever you feel are too bulky to be placed in the business hands of Sayliyah and you want to put them right here because you have a menu of a 10 page document that shows the nonissues grew all when one would reach that billion dollar market in the next two years. If you want to put that then there is a 10 page document you can stick it in the in the marketing plan but it's important enough just in case somebody questions you or to reassure yourself or to read it from time to time so that you know what your market is saying and where you are going with your visit south. That's the appendices and I'll see you in the next chapter. As we begin to round up the business plan.

I Need A Favor Please!

Hi there I know a favorite place if you've got a lot of value from the Book. Could you please post a review. Does that click in the number of stars you think the Book dissolves will be just good enough for now so that when you actually finish the Book then you can go back in and if you want it to last you have the intention to post reviews. But one of the things the co-authors sometimes forget so that's why I'm asking you now to please post the review. Thanks so much. That's what you said.

Recap

We now come to the end of the Book. I showed you the five parts of the business plan executive summary: the marketing plan, the operations plan, and the financial planner. And this is pretty much good to go. So what I have to do is to begin to take action. My a plan as to how you will or write your business plan your business plan does not need to take you two years three years to write although you could tweak your business plan over many years but the first draft of your business plan at least should be done within eight weeks and about three months maximum even if you procrastinate on it in six months time you should look at your business plan.

We also want to do it because you're taking part in this short Book on business planning and will give you a huge discount to get onto my much more elaborate business plan Book. Then check in the bonus chapter below where you find a hugely discounted price that you can get on my eight hour plus Book. All right. Keep me informed and ask me any questions. Enough to go on. Stop putting your business plan together. So I hope to hear from you soon. And remember if you got a value from this kindly write a review. Let's read the names together. I'll see you soon.

5 Ways To Improve Your Cash Flow Forecast

In this chapter I want to talk to you about five ways to improve your cash flow forecast quickly. My name is Bhumi TACA. Let's get started. By way of introduction cash flow is actually the inflow and outflow of money in the business at a particular period and generally when we talk about cash flow we tend to look at it on what happens month by month. Within your business for a period of say 12 months it can be shorter than that Of course and it can be longer than that as well. But we tend to look at cash flow forecasts over a 12 month period to give a really good picture. So what are the five things that you can do that can almost immediately change your cash flow position by changing your cash flow position.

Of course we all know that cash is king and we want to have more cash within our business than going out of it. So how can you create a positive cash flow forecast quickly? So I'll give you five ways. Number one gets paid quicker. The quicker you can get paid the more cash you can have within your business especially if you offer any of these three payment methods that can encourage your clients to pay you quicker i.e. early payment discounts chasing up payments. Another good way of getting paid quicker because sometimes with some businesses the more you chase them up the quicker you get paid.

And I'm not talking about chasing them up in a rude way. I'm talking about chasing them up in a nice way. One of the things I used to do when I was applying products to a particular company was that I knew the head of the admin of that particular place. So whenever she paid me my money I was sent a thank you card that ensured that my invoices went straight up to the top of the power. That's a good thing to do. Also offering cash on delivery discounts can also be a good thing to encourage your clients to pay you quickly. All right. Way number two: what can you do to improve your cash flow forecast. Almost immediately. Well number two is to pay our money out later. You may have to renegotiate terms saying you have a 30 day payment period. You might have to renegotiate that to a 60 day payment period.

So you have money in your business that you are paying out. Also finding new suppliers could be the next thing you might need to do if your current suppliers are being difficult and do not want to extend credit to you as you think you need it then perhaps you jump on the plane go to China and go to Dubai or go to any of those countries where you can get better suppliers that will give you longer payment periods. Also delaying certain purchases can help you to immediately improve your cash flow position. Number three least instead of buying. It's better to lease machinery of vehicles that have to make or outright purchase outright purchases will always cost you money.

Also instead of creating your own software you can lease and build upon an existing software, sort of developing it from scratch which can cost you more money and nothing you can do by way of least but is instead of developing your own software from scratch. Also turn around and do what's called a gay v a joint venture project instead of actually developing from scratch. So that would ensure more cash remains in the business way. Number four pays wages monthly. If you're one of these businesses that is our wages on a weekly basis. Well you want to reach a Gaucher with your employees or your contractors to ensure that you can pay them on a monthly basis because that would save you time.

And that will save you admin costs which means you have more cash remaining in the business. This one strategy can actually put your cash flow in a positive position. Number five generates more cash sales by payment in advance. You can ask your clients to pay in advance if they can't and don't say that's not possible because that's what we do. When I attend seminars we actually pay before we actually attend the seminar so it works. Subscription models could be a good thing. Also selling new products for cash could be a good way to actually improve your cash flow position. So I've given here in this chapter five ways to improve your cash flow forecast quickly and I'll see you with more chapters like this very soon.

An Introduction To Cash Flow Forecasting

Today we're going to be talking about the cash flow forecast. My name is Bhumi Token and I'm from the start of a business academy where we help you build high performance businesses. OK. This is a subject that a lot of people shy away from when it comes to this part of the business which talks about the amount of cash the business has or the amount of money that is flowing in cash into or out of the business. It's an absolutely important part of the business plan. And Of course of the business process and the businesses lifecycle that one needs to pay special attention to the cash flow forecast. And when I'm going to do this series of chapters to actually show you a cash flow forecast template so that we get familiar with it whether you are just starting a business or you're running a business.

It is absolutely important that you have a cash flow forecast that you look at particularly just to make sure you are on the right track and that you are able to meet all the cash demands that you have in the business. All right, by way of introduction, let's say to ourselves why we need to know this. Well number one reason why you know this is that cash flow is the flow of cash into and out of your business within a given period. It's the amount of cash that comes into the business and the amount of cash that leaves the business and then it looks at the difference between both. Okay we could come to the cash flow is the flow of cash into and out of the business. Well why is that important? What's so significant about that?

Well if you're not getting it you're not getting enough cash to meet the outgo waiting that they're going to get into financial difficulty. If Also you're not getting the cash on time with what you need to pay out so you get it in cash this month for let's say the beginning of the month.

You don't get in cash but you need to pay out let's say $10000 or 10000 pounds but you're not going to get that cash to pay it to pay it wait until the end of the middle of the month. Well you're going to have a cash flow. Sure. TH The problem with that is if you keep on having cash flow shortages you'll have to go to somebody.

Normally people go to their bank to try and meet the deficit they have and the cash flow if you do that consistently. The banks are going to look at you as though you don't know what you're doing. So you really want to have a plan to see how I can get into my business with enough money. We're going to deal with it so that you can get enough money for your business. How can we get enough money into the business so that I'm able to meet my outgoings. Very important. The second thing why cash flow is important is because the cash flow is different from the profit and loss account. The amount of sales you see in the cash flow and the amount of turnover on sales that you see in the profit and loss account could be different.

Because let me explain that the profit on loss counts. Generally speaking is the amount of sales that were made in that particular period. So that could be sales made and an invoice is issued. So you come up with a figure because when somebody purchases from you usually one invoice and that invoice issue which is a payment demand so to speak that payment demand that you issue becomes all those payment demands that you issue in a given period say a 12 month period becomes the sales year. The amount of purchases made. And that corresponds with the invoices issued as the sales for the year and the amount of money that you would need to pay out to cover those expenses for the year is your expenses that you deduct the sales from to get you a net profit.

So really a profit loss account is what you might say. The sales you made on paper right now are cash flow though is the actual cash that comes into the business. Let me explain that difference again another way.

When you send an invoice out which is recorded as sales and your profit and loss accounts that invoice may not be paid until 30 or 60 days, sometimes 90 days, sometimes a hundred and twenty days later. So you will have that as sales recorded in your profit and loss account. But you will not have it for cash until the first month if it's 30 days or to the second month if it's 60 days or for the next five months or six months even in some cases. So therefore cash flow is not the same as the sales you generate and the profit loss account.

So it's important to know that because finally cash is king. If you don't have enough cash to meet your expenses it will say that cash is king. Why? If you don't have enough cash to meet your expenses you're going to get in serious financial difficulty. So what we're going to be looking at over the next few chapters is to look at how you can make that cash king of your business. How can you make a task of your business? All right. With that as a way of introduction let's go into this. Let's say that there are three parts to a cash flow forecast and I'm going to show you in a moment what those three packs are on an actual cash Roe focused template that is 2:03 a cash flow forecast. The first part is what I call Level 1 at it. It doesn't mean that everyone I'm calling that level 1 is level 1 which looks at the income that you have in the business.

The second part of the cash flow is the expenses part of it that will show you in a moment. I want to call that level 2 of the cash flow and the third part is the difference between the income and expenses as well as carry over from the previous month's sales. So let me show you what that means. Let me show you on the screen the actual cash flow forecast that I can use to explain to us today or hey you see is a cash flow forecast this part of it we have them. My mouse is moving on. Oh by the way let me explain this for us. OK. On this first column other items which is the list of either sales types appear or receive low income types here receipts or income types and the expenses the payment types on that column on that column there and then down here are the differences.

So if you go back up Level one is the amount of income all types of income generated over a 12 month period. Now you can do a cash flow for a month and you can do a cash flow for three months get a cash flow for six months cash or for 12 months. It does depend. Generally speaking though it's better to do a cash flow for a 12 months period. A better picture of what your business will look like. All right now this part of it that I'm holding on the left is what I call Level 1. It's really the research part of the income part of the cash flow forecast. Now what I call Level 2 is down here and this is the expense. It's part of your cash flow forecast. And then what I call Level 3 is the differences between your expenses and your sales as it relates with the actual balances at the end of each month.

So when are we actually going to put some figures as we go along to use that to explain to you a cash flow in a better way. So now the. So the first column is the items. The second column tends to be what's called the pre-start process or the pre. So the pre-start period which is before you actually started trading you might have introduced a certain amount of money in. So let's put 10000. Whether you're working with a dollar or pounds doesn't mean it makes a difference or you might have received a loan as well to start your business with the same sort of level of 10000 as well. Okay. So we've got a 10000 loan and 10000 capital the amount of money we invested into the business. Notice that there were no sales and we're going to talk about that pretty soon now. The beautiful thing about this template is that it automatically calculates for you.

The figures that you put into the template itself. So if you come down here it's automatically calculated for you the amount of money you had and you know since you didn't spend anything yet it's still got that balance carried over our balance to the. So you really need this kind of template. Say if you email me to Bhumi to start your own business I can let you come to Bhoomi. Start Your Own Business Academy dot com. I'll email you this template so that you can use it for your business too. All right so let's recap on some of the things we've said today. Let's recap them to the day. The PowerPoint. Just to recap what we have discussed today already. OK.

Now what we said was cash flows are pretty important and we look at the need to know why cash is important cash flows in and out of cash in the business. And it is different from a profit loss. And cash is king. Also we talked about the cash for having three different levels of three different portions to it. The first part is the income or research level. Second part is the payment expenses level and the third part is the differences between the income and expenses. And then it carries over some of the figures for the previous month onto the next month. Don't worry when we start putting in some figures it makes better sense for us right now.

Let me let me stop on this and say before we before we start going on with this cash flow let me say something to that just because you put in absolutely important they need to be as realistic to your niche as possible so don't pluck figures from the air and just put it in there and say well you know that's why I'm going to do it because because that won't work for your business that you've got to put in figures that you generated as a result of research if you are just starting a business you do not have what we can call historical figures because you've not traded before. So what you can have is research figures. So you've looked at your competitors and you've spoken to your potential customers. You've kind of done some research that informs you.

All of you are likely to sell your possible expenses and stuff so you need to have those figures. I once saw a cash flow for a music business this person in their cash flow. I was brought into a room by my boss who told me to have a look at this cash for focus because I wanted to give the person some money. The cash flows said that in the first month they are going to sell something like 5000 units of a release. Then the next month they're going to sell about 20000 of the release anyway. By time they went down to 12 the cash flow suggests that they were making a million sales a month in that month.

Or they would have made a million sales in total for the year. Now I read the business plan briefly in my boss's office and I said don't give them the money because there's no other work or someone said Well how do you know that he asked me out. Well the point is they've not made them have no experience in generating sales at all. For example in the music business if you don't have experience in generating sales to think that you're going to generate a million sales in a year it's just completely ridiculous. It's just not the way it works. So it's considering the fact that 95 percent of releases today will sell 100 copies. That's the industry figures 95 percent of releases do not sell 100 copies. So are you going to make a million sales in the first year?

Well as somebody said well if you are signed to a major label or you could make that sell. That's true. That's the only way it could happen. It could happen you know generally speaking I said why it can't go viral. Everybody thinks that their products are going to go viral. That's not the way to run a business. You have to run a business in a sensible way and in a way that builds your business as you go along. So whatever business you're doing please ensure that the figures you put into your cash flow forecast whether you're a hairdresser what they can and whether you're a plumber whether you're an electrician whether you are a psychologist or whether you are a fitness trainer or whatever you are you've got to put in figures that come from well research sources.

All right, let's see what we're going to stop. And you can get in touch with me like I said I would love to give you this template that you can use for your business for free. Don't do it for free. So just email me at Start Your Own Business Academy dot com and you can go to my Website and pick up one of my books for free called How to Start Your Own Business in

30 days and begin making profits. All right. I'll speak to you soon as we go over to Pat to some other chapters in the series. God bless.

How To Close More Sales

Hi there, welcome to the final chapter from our series for Quick Fixes to improve yourself. My name is Boomi Token and if you are here for the first time, do subscribe to the channel. All right. Let's get straight into it. We've covered existing customer strategy. That was the first chapter. Second chapter was a point of sale strategy. The third chapter was immediately after the sales strategy. And today, the final chapter we're going to cover improving four major elements, one of the four major elements you need to improve to kind of bring this whole series together to help you really boost your sales straight away. I want to give you what they are that I'm going to go into the details of for each one of them. The first thing you need to do is around your target market, really scrutinizing your target market.

Number two headlines, number three, differentiator. And number four, social proof. OK, that's going to each one in a little bit more detail. No one is really getting down into the nitty gritty of choosing a target market when we talk about choosing a target market. A lot of people think they're going to lose out on sales if they don't, you know, if they don't appeal to everybody. The point is, even Coca-Cola, as big as that brand of Coca-Cola, is a huge brand. They don't appeal to every single person. I bet you the audience, the target market is wrong about the 16 to 24 years old. I mean, that's what I think the target market is. If you think about products like even the iPad or the Apple products, they appeal to a particular audience.

People who are really into Samsung don't buy Apple products and people who are really into Apple, hey, they run away from Samsung products. That's to tell you that we all need to target. So you need to target people who want your product. Not only did I not need it, I said I wanted your product. There's a difference between needing it and wanting it. A lot of people need many things, but they don't want them, so they don't get them. So they must want a product, people who want your product or services, people who can afford to pay for your product or services, people who can be easily reached because they are easily identifiable. And then finally, people who have similar attributes.

So you need to pick a specific target market, narrow down to your target market if you've worked in a target market before. And you think, OK, just hearing you now speak, I need to do something. Yeah. You need to even retarget your market. Here's the deal. You cannot target every single person because the messages that appeal to different target markets have to be delivered to them. You cannot deliver the same message to everybody and think that, oh, it's just going to work that way. No, it's not going to work that way. OK, let me give you this quick example.

I learned from Steve, Steve Hackney in this example, Steve actually said, OK, you start a business and you are looking to employ an accountant to help you, but you're a startup, right? OK, and then you look at these two ads, the first ad says, hi there. This is a big accounting firm and we specialize in auditing, keeping the books and helping you to establish structure. OK, and the second ad says this is a B.S. accounting firm. We specialize in helping small businesses get up and start quickly profitably and with the right structure. Guess what? Who is more appealing to you as a startup, Of course, is the second ad. That's the kind of thing that I'm talking about. So you have to target your market and target the message that you deliver to them. All right.

Second thing is about differentiators. What is your differentiator? You know, if you think about Domino's Pizza, Domino's Pizza will deliver within half an hour. That was a differentiator. They weren't talking about that. Domino's Pizza was the best pizza since sliced bread. No, they weren't saying that. They were simply saying they've targeted an audience, which is a student, and when they want to eat the one eight right now.

So we're going to make sure we get your food to you right now. That was the differentiator. So you need to have a differentiator. What makes it different from your competitors? Not only have it, but you should communicate it at every opportunity, communicating your flyers, communicating your letters, communicating and keep communicating to your target market.

Number three, what you need to improve is your headlines. Remember the newspapers. When you go past a newsstand, you always read the headlines. If the headlines grab you, then you are likely to stop and read the whole story. If the headline doesn't grab you, nobody goes to a news headline. I start looking for stories. No, you look for the headline and if the headline works, then you look at the story. So this is kind of how two headlines always work. But one thing I would tell you is if you sign up to Google and you go to the AdWords section and you do the searches, you can use searchable phrases as headlines. But whatever it is, your headlines need to grab your target market. And then finally, number four is social proof.

You need to use social proof in all your communications, use it on your flyers, use it in your letters, use it. Just keep using it, because social proof is what other people have said about you and people or your audience, your customers, your clients. They want to know what people have said about you and that. Gives you credibility when you communicate it all right? Those are the four things that you need to improve. If you do that together, then you're going to benefit from exponential sales and exponential difference in your sales and marketing efforts. OK, I've been using CONCETTINA and the other chapters. I've been using an online tool called Sales Accelerator Roadmap. Sales Accelerator Roadmap.

You put in some details about your sales and what you're doing right now, and it would spit out to you your weaknesses, your opportunities and the steps you need to take to actually improve and get to your goals. It's really good. It's really helped me. So I'm giving it to you for now for free by going to my website, which is w w w dot business mandate coaching dot com w w w dot business mandate coaching dot com. If you go back to that website right now, you sign up for it and you'll be able to use it for free at the moment. So let's recap what we talked about in this chapter. In this chapter, we've talked about improving the four elements. What are the four elements? Improving your target, marketing, communicating your differentiator, using good headlines and communicating the social proof that you have generated from your clients. OK.

Remember, the link to the other three chapters are going to be in the description below. I've talked in those chapters about how to improve your sales using your existing customer strategy point of sale strategy immediately after sales strategy. And today we talked about improving the four core elements or the four major elements. If you're using any type of strategy that is working for you, please, please, please put it in the comments below so that other people can also learn from you. Remember, go back to my chapter, go over to my website, and I'll chapter my website and access the sales accelerator roadmap that's going to help you grow your sales.

And marketing is basically going to add a lot more to what I've been communicating to you and give you the practical steps as well that you can take to improve your sales. It is at WWE Business Mandate Coaching dot com. All right. If you like this chapter, do subscribe to the channel, do like it and do share it. All right, then, until I see you again in another series soon. I'll speak to you soon. Thank you. This is Boomi. Token your encouragement. Come on, go and encourage somebody. God bless.

What Next

Hi there! I'm so excited today because if you've been part of my Books, you will know that I've dedicated my time to help you learn and also to help you grow. So today I have something extra special for you. Whether you're thinking about starting your entrepreneurial journey or you want to start scaling up your business, here are the two things that I have for you. Number one is my 1 to 1 consultancy. If you are thinking about starting a business, we can meet and talk about how to test and validate your business idea, how to secure your first client, how to raise capital for the venture that you want to do, and lots more that we're going to share in that one hour. But if you're thinking about also growing your business, though, if that's the state that you're at, we would come up with personalized growth strategies.

Uncover your business goldmine, and explore some innovative ways in which you can raise money for your scaling. And this is all about helping you to unlock your full potential. We'll also answer all the questions that you have and areas that you think are cloudy that you kind of want some clarity on will help you to do that in that hour for the 1 to 1 consulting. So the best part of this is that every month we are offering a 50% off a 50% discount to anyone who wants to come on our 1 to 1 consulting, one person a month. You pay only $75. And if you miss out on that because you did not apply on time, then you gotta pay. The going rate right now is $150 per hour for the consultant.

So the second offer that I have for you, though, is to come onto my online learning subscription on this online learning subscription, what I plan to do is to put a load of my Books onto this website, where you can access for $7 a month for $7 a month. Yeah, and you'll be able to cancel at any time, and you will gain access for as long as you're subscribing to that particular channel. So whether you want to learn about digital marketing or you want to learn entrepreneurship, or you want to learn business planning, or you want to learn how to, uh, get referrals, how to create a referral system, whatever it is. And the good thing is that I've dedicated the Books to be specifically designed for those who are earning under £100,000.

So if that's you yet, then you want to come on that. So those are my two offers that I have for you today. The 1 to 1. Consulting. Whether you are thinking of starting a business or scaling your business, we can meet and talk online and we will help you to do that. That is $75 if you get our discounted rate or $150. So. Here is time for you to take action. Or the second offer, therefore, is to come on to this subscription, uh, where you find a lot of my Books on there for $7 a month and you can cancel anytime. So that's what I have for you today, because I want to help you to either scale your business or grow your business at an affordable price. So take a look at the description below, and you'll find some, uh, information on how you can get in touch. All right. I look forward to talking to you soon. And, um, have a great day. Thank you.